# Pocket Guide To Artificial Intelligence

Henrik Envall

ISBN: 9798858070719

# CONTENTS

# Introduction to Artificial Intelligence

**The Dawn of Thought Machines**

Imagine a world where machines can think, reason, and even dream. A world where they can understand human emotions, compose music, paint masterpieces, and solve complex problems that baffle even the brightest human minds. This isn't a scene from a sci-fi movie; this is the world of Artificial Intelligence (AI).

**What is Artificial Intelligence?**

At its core, AI is the science of making machines intelligent. But what does "intelligent" mean? For humans, intelligence encompasses a range of abilities - from recognizing patterns and making decisions to understanding complex concepts and learning from experience. In the realm of AI, it means creating algorithms that allow machines to perform tasks that typically require human intelligence. Whether it's Siri understanding your voice commands, Tesla's self-driving cars navigating the streets, or a chess program defeating a grandmaster, AI is the brain behind these feats.

**A Brief Stroll Down Memory Lane**

The dream of creating intelligent machines isn't new. Ancient myths from various cultures speak of statues that could come to life or mechanical men with human-like qualities. However, the scientific journey of AI began in the mid-20th century. The term "Artificial Intelligence" was coined in 1955 by John McCarthy for the famous Dartmouth Conference, the birthplace of AI as an academic discipline.

Over the decades, AI has seen highs and lows. There were periods of extreme optimism, where it seemed machines would soon possess human-like intelligence, followed by "AI winters" - periods of skepticism and reduced funding. But with the advent of big data, powerful computing, and advanced algorithms in the 21st century, AI has witnessed an unprecedented resurgence.

**AI, ML, DL: Decoding the Acronyms**

As you delve deeper into AI, you'll encounter terms like Machine Learning (ML) and Deep Learning (DL). While they're often used interchangeably with AI, they're subsets of it. Think of AI as the vast universe of intelligent computing. ML is a galaxy within this universe, where machines learn from data. DL, on the other hand, is a planet within the ML galaxy, inspired by the human brain's neural networks.

# Why AI Matters

## More Than Just Machines Thinking

Artificial Intelligence is not just a buzzword or a futuristic concept; it's a transformative force reshaping our world. The implications of AI stretch far beyond just technology. It's about enhancing human capabilities, solving complex problems, and creating a world of possibilities that were once deemed science fiction. Let's delve deeper into why AI is so pivotal in today's age.

## Healthcare: Diagnosis to Treatment

In the realm of healthcare, AI is a game-changer. Machine learning algorithms can analyze medical images with precision, often detecting anomalies that might be missed by the human eye. For instance, Google's DeepMind has developed an AI that can spot eye diseases in scans, potentially saving patients from blindness. Beyond diagnostics, AI-powered robots assist surgeons in intricate procedures, ensuring higher precision and quicker recovery times. Moreover, personalized treatment plans based on genetic information are becoming a reality, thanks to AI's data-crunching capabilities.

## Environment: Earth's New Best Friend

Our planet faces unprecedented challenges, from climate change to deforestation. AI comes to the rescue by analyzing vast datasets to predict environmental changes, track endangered species, and optimize renewable energy sources. For instance, AI algorithms monitor satellite images to detect deforestation in real-time, enabling quicker interventions.

## Finance: Smarter Money Management

The financial sector is reaping the benefits of AI in myriad ways. Fraud detection has become more robust, with AI systems analyzing millions of transactions in real-time to spot suspicious activities. Robo-advisors, powered by AI, provide personalized investment advice to users, democratizing access to financial planning. Furthermore, AI-driven algorithms predict stock market trends with increasing accuracy, aiding investment strategies.

### Entertainment: Personalized Experiences

Ever wondered how Netflix or Spotify always seem to know what you're in the mood for? Thank AI for that. These platforms use machine learning to analyze your preferences and viewing history, curating personalized recommendations. In the world of gaming, AI-driven characters adapt to your playing style, making games more immersive and challenging.

### Transportation: The Future is Autonomous

The dream of self-driving cars is inching closer to reality, all thanks to AI. Advanced algorithms process data from vehicle sensors in real-time, making split-second decisions that can help avoid accidents and navigate the roads. Beyond cars, AI-driven drones and autonomous ships are set to revolutionize transportation and logistics.

### Education: Tailored Learning

AI is transforming education by offering personalized learning experiences. Intelligent tutoring systems adapt content in real-time based on a student's performance, ensuring that each learner gets a tailored experience. Furthermore, AI-driven platforms can help educators identify students who might be at risk, enabling timely interventions.

# Foundations of Machine Learning

**The Magic Behind the Machine**

Have you ever wondered how your email filters out spam? Or how your favorite music app seems to know your taste in songs so well? The answer lies in the realm of Machine Learning (ML). But before we dive into the intricacies, let's demystify what ML really is.

**What is Machine Learning?**

Machine Learning is a subset of Artificial Intelligence that allows computers to learn from data. Instead of being explicitly programmed to perform a task, these machines use algorithms and statistical models to identify patterns, make decisions, and improve their performance over time. In essence, ML is about teaching computers to learn from experience.

**Common Types of Machine Learning**

**Supervised Learning:** This is akin to a student-teacher scenario. The algorithm (student) is trained on a labeled dataset, where the answer (or output) is known. The goal is to learn a mapping from inputs to outputs. Once trained, the algorithm can predict the output for new, unseen data. Examples include email spam filters and credit score predictions.

**Unsupervised Learning:** Here, the algorithm is like an explorer. It's given data without explicit instructions on what to do with it. The goal is to find patterns or structures in the data. Common techniques include clustering (grouping similar data points) and dimensionality reduction (simplifying data without losing its essence). Market segmentation in business is a classic example.

**Reinforcement Learning:** Imagine training a dog. It performs an action, and based on that action, it either gets a treat (reward) or doesn't. Over time, the dog learns to perform actions that maximize its rewards. Similarly, in reinforcement learning, algorithms learn by interacting with an environment and receiving feedback in the form of rewards or penalties.

## Key Concepts in ML

**Dataset:** A collection of data used to train, validate, or test a machine learning model. It's the raw material that fuels ML algorithms.

**Features:** These are the input variables that the algorithm uses to make predictions. For instance, in predicting house prices, features might include the number of bedrooms, location, and size of the house.

**Model:** Once an algorithm is trained on a dataset, it results in a model. This model can then be used to make predictions on new data.

**Overfitting & Underfitting:** Striking the right balance is crucial in ML. Overfitting occurs when a model is too complex and performs exceptionally well on training data but poorly on new data. Underfitting is the opposite, where the model is too simple to capture the underlying patterns in the data.

**Evaluation Metrics:** Once a model is trained, how do we know it's good? Metrics like accuracy, precision, recall, and F1 score help in evaluating a model's performance.

## Why Machine Learning Matters

Machine Learning is the engine driving the AI revolution. From healthcare diagnostics and financial forecasting to voice assistants and recommendation systems, ML algorithms are at the heart of these innovations. They offer the promise of automating routine tasks, providing insights from vast amounts of data, and introducing new ways of solving age-old problems.

# AI Algorithms. The Engines Driving Intelligent Systems

## Decoding the Intelligence in Artificial Intelligence

At the heart of every AI system lies a set of algorithms, specifically designed to mimic, replicate, or even surpass human intelligence. These algorithms, grouped into distinct families based on their functionalities, serve as the foundation for various AI applications we encounter daily. Let's take a closer look at these algorithms to understand how they fit in the AI landscape.

### 1. Supervised Learning Algorithms

#### Linear Regression:

> **Description:** Predicts a continuous value based on input features.

> **Use Case:** Predicting house prices based on area, number of rooms, etc.

#### Decision Trees:

> **Description:** Makes decisions based on asking a series of questions.

> **Use Case:** Medical diagnosis based on symptoms.

#### Support Vector Machines (SVM):

> **Description:** Classifies data into categories by finding the optimal separating hyperplane.

> **Use Case:** Image classification tasks.

### 2. Unsupervised Learning Algorithms

#### K-Means Clustering:

**Description:** Groups data into 'k' number of clusters based on feature similarity.

**Use Case:** Market segmentation for targeted advertising.

### Hierarchical Clustering:

**Description:** Builds a tree of clusters by successively merging or splitting groups.

**Use Case:** Taxonomy creation in biology.

### Principal Component Analysis (PCA):

**Description:** Reduces the dimensionality of data by preserving as much variability as possible.

**Use Case:** Data visualization and noise reduction.

## 3. Neural Networks and Deep Learning

### Convolutional Neural Networks (CNN):

**Description:** Processes data with a grid-like topology, such as an image.

**Use Case:** Image and video recognition.

### Recurrent Neural Networks (RNN):

**Description:** Processes sequences of data by looping outputs back into inputs.

**Use Case:** Speech recognition and time series prediction.

### Generative Adversarial Networks (GAN):

**Description:** Consists of two networks, one generating data and the other evaluating it.

**Use Case:** Art creation and image super-resolution.

## 4. Reinforcement Learning Algorithms

### Q-Learning:

**Description:** Learns an action policy based on the notion of maximizing rewards over time.

**Use Case:** Game playing, like training agents to play chess.

### Deep Q Network (DQN):

**Description:** Combines Q-learning with deep neural networks.

**Use Case:** Complex tasks like playing video games.

### Policy Gradients:

**Description:** Optimizes the policy of an agent directly through gradient ascent.

**Use Case:** Robotics and real-time decision-making.

## 5. Natural Language Processing Algorithms

### Bag of Words (BoW):

**Description:** Represents text data by the frequency of words, disregarding order and grammar.

**Use Case:** Text classification and sentiment analysis.

### Word Embeddings (e.g., Word2Vec):

**Description:** Represents words in a dense vector space where similar words are close to each other.

**Use Case:** Semantic search and recommendation systems.

### Transformers:

**Description:** Processes input data in parallel (rather than sequentially) and captures long-range dependencies.

**Use Case:** Machine translation and text summarization.

## Why is an algorithm considered AI?

When we hear the term "Artificial Intelligence," we often think of humanoid robots, self-driving cars, or sophisticated natural language processing systems like chatbots. These are the poster children of AI, showcasing the field's incredible potential to mimic or even surpass human capabilities. However, this glamorous portrayal can sometimes overshadow the more humble, yet equally important, algorithms that form the backbone of AI. One such example is linear regression, a statistical method that seems almost too simple to be categorized under the AI umbrella.

**The Simplicity of Linear Regression**

Linear regression is a straightforward algorithm that aims to model the relationship between two variables by fitting a linear equation to observed data. For example, it can predict a student's final grade based on the number of hours they've studied. The algorithm is simple, interpretable, and has been around for centuries. So, why is it considered AI?

**The Complexity of Neural Networks and NLP**

On the other end of the spectrum, we have neural networks and natural language processing (NLP) algorithms. Neural networks are inspired by the human brain and consist of interconnected nodes or "neurons." They can learn from data and make complex decisions, making them ideal for tasks like image recognition, language translation, and even playing video games. NLP algorithms, particularly those based on transformer architectures, can understand, generate, and respond to human language in a way that was once thought to be the exclusive domain of humans.

**Bridging the Gap**

The key to understanding why both linear regression and neural networks fall under the AI umbrella lies in the definition of AI itself. AI is not solely about mimicking human intelligence or complexity; it's about creating machines that can perform tasks that would ordinarily require human intelligence. In that sense, even a "simple" algorithm like linear regression is a form of AI because it automates a task—data prediction—that humans would otherwise have to do manually.

Moreover, not all problems require the computational firepower of neural networks or the linguistic finesse of NLP algorithms. Sometimes, a simple linear regression model is more than sufficient, and using a more complex model could lead to overfitting or unnecessary computational costs.

**The Role of Perception**

Public perception plays a significant role in how we categorize algorithms. The media often focuses on the most groundbreaking advancements in AI, which usually involve neural networks, deep learning, or NLP. This focus can create a perception gap, making it hard to see how simpler algorithms fit into the AI landscape. However, it's essential to recognize that AI is a broad field with a wide range of tools, each with its own strengths, weaknesses, and ideal use-cases.

## In Conclusion

AI algorithms, with their diverse functionalities and applications, are the linchpins of modern intelligent systems. They empower machines to see, hear, speak, and make decisions, bridging the gap between human capabilities and computational prowess. As AI continues to evolve, these algorithms will undoubtedly play an even more pivotal role in shaping the future of technology.

# Regression analysis in Machine Learning

## The Essence of Regression

At the heart of regression lies a simple quest: to predict a continuous outcome based on one or more input variables. Whether it's forecasting sales for the next quarter or predicting the temperature for tomorrow, regression provides the tools to make these predictions with confidence.

## Linear Regression: The Starting Point

Linear regression, the cornerstone of regression techniques, seeks to establish a linear relationship between the input and output variables. Imagine plotting data points on a graph and then drawing the straightest line that best fits those points. This line, represented by the equation $y=mx+c$, is the essence of linear regression.

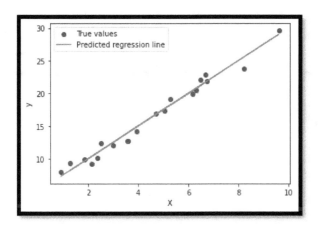

**Venturing Beyond Linearity: Polynomial Regression**

Life isn't always linear, and neither is data. For those curvy, nonlinear patterns, polynomial regression comes to the rescue. Instead of a straight line, it fits a curve, capturing the nuances and intricacies of the data. The equation might look a bit more complex, like $y=ax^3+bx^2+cx+d$, but the principle remains the same: find the best fit.

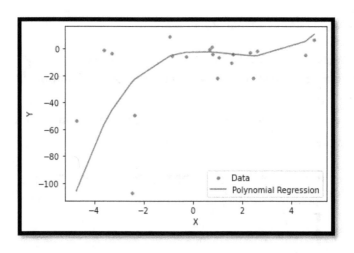

**Regularization: Ridge and Lasso Regression**

In the world of high-dimensional data, where features often correlate, Ridge and Lasso regression emerge as heroes. These techniques introduce a penalty, ensuring that the model doesn't become overly complex and overfit the training data. While Ridge adds a squared penalty, Lasso goes a step further, potentially setting some feature coefficients to zero, effectively performing feature selection.

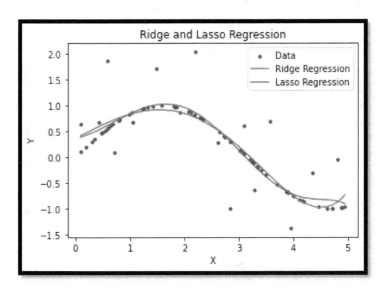

## A Twist in the Tale: Logistic Regression

Logistic regression might sound like a regression algorithm, but it's a master of binary classification. At its core is the sigmoid function, mapping any value to a range between 0 and 1, perfect for estimating probabilities.

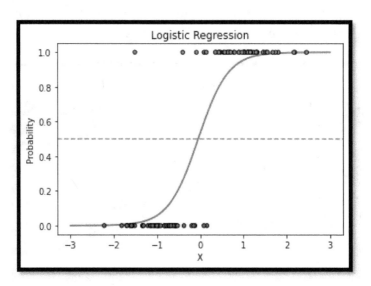

## The Mathematics Behind Regression

Regression analysis is fundamentally rooted in mathematics, and understanding its underlying principles provides clarity on how predictions are made.

The primary objective of regression is to minimize the difference, or error, between predicted and actual values. This error quantifies how far off our predictions are from the actual data points. The goal is to reduce this error to ensure the model's accuracy.

One of the foundational techniques used in regression is the method of least squares. Developed by the mathematician Carl Friedrich Gauss, this method calculates the best-fitting line or curve by minimizing the sum of the squared differences between observed values and those predicted by the model.

Ridge and Lasso regression introduce further mathematical refinements to the regression process. These techniques incorporate a penalty term to the standard regression equation. The purpose of this penalty is to prevent overfitting, a scenario where the model is too closely aligned with the training data and may perform poorly on new, unseen data.

In logistic regression, used primarily for classification tasks, the sigmoid function plays a crucial role. This function ensures that any input is transformed into a value between 0 and 1, suitable for estimating probabilities.

In essence, regression is a systematic approach to understanding and interpreting data patterns. Through mathematical equations and techniques, it provides a structured way to make informed predictions based on data.

## Decision Trees

Imagine you're playing a game of 20 questions. Each question you ask is designed to narrow down the possibilities until you can make an educated guess. In essence, this is how a Decision Tree works in the world of computer algorithms.

**What is a Decision Tree?**

A Decision Tree is like a flowchart where each decision leads you down a different path. It starts with a single box (or "node") that represents a question about some data. Depending on the answer, you follow a branch to another node, which represents another question, and so on, until you reach an answer at the end.

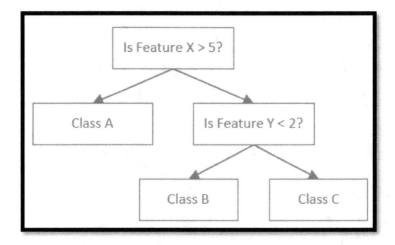

**Breaking it Down**

> **Questions (Decision Nodes):** These are the points where a decision is made. For example, "Is it raining outside?"

**Answers (Branches):** These are the paths leading from one question to another, or to a final answer.

**Final Answers (Leaf Nodes):** These are the end points of the tree where no further questions are asked.

## Why are Decision Trees Useful?

**Simplicity:** Just like a flowchart, Decision Trees are easy to follow. You start at the top and work your way down, making decisions along the way.

**Versatility:** They can be used for various tasks, like deciding if an email is spam or not, predicting house prices, or recommending movies.

**Visual:** They can be drawn out and visualized, making them easy to understand, even if you're not a computer whiz.

## Mathematical Foundations

At its core, a Decision Tree uses mathematical formulas to decide which questions to ask and in what order. Here's a glimpse into the math behind it:

1. **Entropy:** This is a measure of randomness or unpredictability. In the context of Decision Trees, it helps determine how mixed the data is. A set of data with all similar items has low entropy, while a mixed set has high entropy.

*Formula:* $E(S) = -p_+ \log_2(p_+) - p_- \log_2(p_-)$ where $p_+$ and $p_-$ are the proportions of positive and negative examples in a data set $S$.

2. **Information Gain:** This measures how much uncertainty is reduced after splitting the data based on a particular attribute. The attribute that results in the highest information gain is chosen for the decision.

*Formula:* $IG(S,A) = E(S) - \sum_{v \in Values(A)} (|S_v|/|S|) E(S_v)$ where $S$ is the current dataset, $A$ is an attribute, and $S_v$ is the subset of $S$ for which attribute $A$ has value $v$.

## Some Challenges

While Decision Trees are powerful, they're not perfect. If they ask too many questions, they might get too specific, making correct decisions only for the examples they've seen and failing with new ones. This is like playing 20 questions but insisting on asking 100!

## In Everyday Life

Imagine you're deciding what to wear. Your Decision Tree might start with, "Is it cold outside?" If yes, you might choose a sweater; if no, maybe a t-shirt. Next, "Is it a formal event?" If yes, add a nice jacket, and so on. This process of making decisions based on conditions is the essence of a Decision Tree.

In conclusion, Decision Trees are a way for computers to make decisions by asking a series of questions. They're a bit like a game of 20 questions, guiding the computer to the right answer, one step at a time.

# Support Vector Machines

Trying to separate two groups of things with a straight line, ensuring that the line is as far away from both groups as possible. This is the essence of Support Vector Machines (SVM), a powerful tool in the machine learning toolkit.

**What is a Support Vector Machine?**

At its core, an SVM is like a divider. Given data points that belong to one of two categories, SVM finds the best line (or in more complex cases, a plane or hyperplane) that separates these categories. The magic of SVM is in how it determines the "best" line: it's the one that maintains the maximum distance from any data point, ensuring a clear margin of separation.

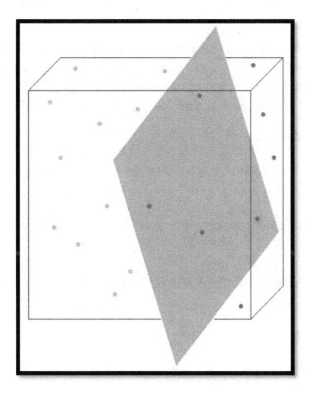

**Diving into the Math**

While the concept sounds simple, there's intricate math at play:

1.  **Margin:** This is the distance between the separating line (or hyperplane) and the nearest data point from either group. The goal of SVM is to maximize this margin. The data points that touch the edges of this margin are called "support vectors."

2.  **Hyperplane:** In a 2-dimensional space, the separator is a line. In 3D, it's a plane, and in higher dimensions, it's called a hyperplane. Mathematically, it's represented as:

    $w \cdot x + b = 0$ where $w$ is the weight vector and $b$ is the bias.

3.  **Optimization:** SVMs use quadratic programming to find the values of $w$ and $b$ that maximize the margin. This involves solving a set of equations that minimize a quadratic function subject to some constraints.

4.  **Kernel Trick:** For data that isn't linearly separable, SVMs use a trick called the "kernel trick" to transform the data into a higher dimension where it becomes separable. Common kernels include polynomial, radial basis function (RBF), and sigmoid.

**Why are SVMs Valued?**

**Robustness:** SVMs are effective even when the number of dimensions is greater than the number of samples.

**Flexibility:** With the kernel trick, SVMs can handle non-linear data, making them versatile.

**Accuracy:** They often provide high accuracy rates and are less prone to overfitting.

**Challenges:**

**Scalability:** For large datasets, SVMs can be computationally intensive.

**Choice of Kernel:** The selection of the right kernel function can be tricky and is crucial for the SVM's performance.

**Everyday Analogy**

Imagine you're at a park, and you see two groups of animals: cats on one side and dogs on the other. You want to draw a line on the ground that keeps the two groups separate, ensuring that the line is as far from any cat or dog as possible. This is what SVM does, but in a more mathematical and precise manner.

In conclusion, Support Vector Machines combine intuitive principles with advanced mathematics to classify data effectively. They're like the precise dividers of the machine learning world, ensuring clear boundaries between categories.

# Clustering Algorithms, Unveiling Hidden Patterns

In the vast universe of data, patterns often lie hidden, waiting to be discovered. Clustering algorithms in machine learning are like cosmic telescopes, revealing groups and structures within data that might not be immediately visible to the naked eye.

**Introduction to Clustering**

At its heart, clustering is about grouping. In machine learning, clustering algorithms seek to partition a dataset into subsets (clusters), ensuring that data points in the same subset are similar while being distinct from points in other subsets. It's an unsupervised learning technique, meaning it doesn't rely on pre-labeled data.

**Main Types of Clustering Algorithms**

1.  **K-Means Clustering:**

    **Principle:** Partition the data into 'K' clusters by minimizing the distance between data points and their assigned centroids.

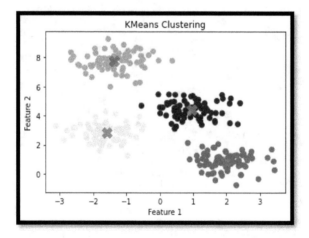

2. **Hierarchical Clustering:**

**Principle:** Build a tree-like structure (dendrogram) to represent data hierarchies. Data points can be grouped by cutting the dendrogram at a desired level.

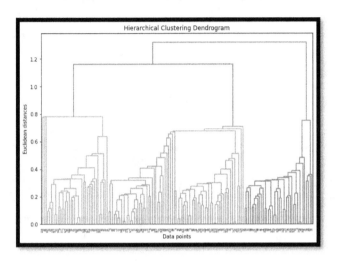

3. **DBSCAN:**

> **Principle:** Focus on density. Points in dense regions form clusters, while those in sparser areas are treated as outliers.

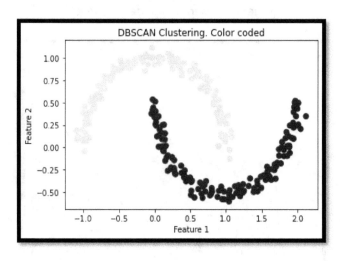

4. **Agglomerative Clustering:**

> **Principle:** A bottom-up approach where each data point starts as an individual cluster, and pairs of clusters merge as one moves up the hierarchy.

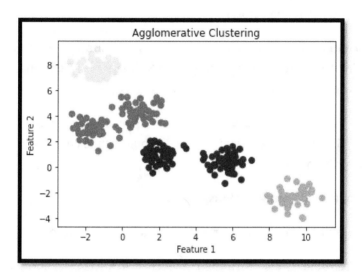

In the last example you can clearly see how the number of clusters visible in the data is not equal to the number of clusters used in the clustering algorithm. It shows the importance of adapting the parameters of the algorithm to match the data.

## Diving Deeper: The Mathematics Behind

**Distance Metrics:** The essence of clustering lies in measuring distances. Common metrics include Euclidean (straight-line distance), Manhattan (sum of absolute differences), and cosine (angle between vectors) distances.

**Optimization:** Clustering often involves optimization tasks, like minimizing intra-cluster distances in K-Means or maximizing inter-cluster distances.

**Validity Indices:** How do we know if our clusters are good? Indices like Silhouette Coefficient or Davies-Bouldin Index provide quantitative measures of cluster quality.

## Challenges and Considerations

**Scalability:** Some algorithms struggle with large datasets.

**Determining Cluster Number:** Especially in K-Means, choosing the right 'K' is crucial.

**High Dimensionality:** As data dimensions increase, distance metrics can become less meaningful, a phenomenon known as the "curse of dimensionality."

## Real-world Analogies

Imagine you're a librarian with thousands of books but no categories. Clustering is like intuitively organizing these books into sections based on their content, themes, and styles, even if the genres aren't explicitly labeled.

## Conclusion

Clustering algorithms in machine learning are powerful tools that bring structure to unstructured data. They're like the cartographers of the data world, mapping out the terrain and revealing the hidden landscapes within. Whether you're a business looking to understand customer behavior or a scientist seeking patterns in complex datasets, clustering is an invaluable asset in the quest for knowledge.

# Neural Networks and Deep Learning

## The Brain Behind the Machine

Imagine trying to replicate the intricate workings of the human brain, with its billions of neurons and trillions of connections, in a machine. This ambitious idea forms the foundation of neural networks and deep learning. Let's embark on a journey to understand the magic behind these powerful AI tools.

## What are Neural Networks?

Neural Networks (NN) are computational models inspired by the human brain's structure. Just as our brain consists of neurons interconnected by synapses, neural networks comprise layers of nodes (analogous to neurons) connected by "weights" (akin to synapses). These networks are designed to recognize patterns by processing data through these layers.

## The Anatomy of a Neural Network:

**Input Layer:** This is where the network receives data. Each node in this layer corresponds to a feature in the data.

**Hidden Layers:** These are layers between the input and output. They process and transform the data, extracting complex patterns.

**Output Layer:** This layer produces the final prediction or classification based on the processed data.

**Deep Learning: Diving Deeper**

When neural networks have a large number of hidden layers, they're termed as "Deep Neural Networks." The field of studying these networks is known as Deep Learning (DL). The "depth" allows these networks to learn and represent more complex functions and patterns.

**Why "Deep" Matters:** Deep networks can automatically learn feature hierarchies. For instance, in image recognition, initial layers might recognize edges, the next layers identify shapes by combining edges, and even further layers might recognize complex structures like faces or objects.

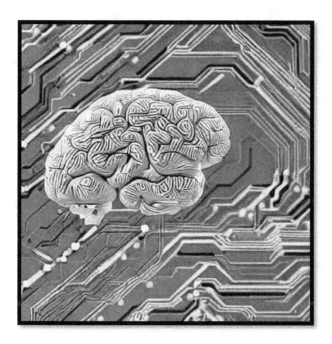

**Deep Neural Network Structure:**

**Input Layer (Green):** This is where the network receives data. Each node in this layer corresponds to a feature in the data.

**Hidden Layers:** These are layers between the input and output. They process and transform the data, extracting complex patterns. In our visual representation, we have three hidden layers, but deep neural networks can have many more.

**Output Layer (Red):** This layer produces the final prediction or classification based on the processed data.

The connections between the layers represent the "weights" that adjust as the network learns from data. The beauty of neural networks lies in their ability to learn and adapt, making them a cornerstone of modern AI.

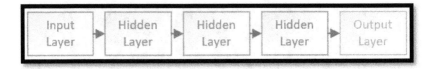

## Types of Neural Networks:

**Feedforward Neural Networks:** The most basic type where information moves in one direction—from input to output.

**Convolutional Neural Networks (CNNs):** Tailored for image processing, CNNs have specialized layers that can automatically detect features in images.

**Recurrent Neural Networks (RNNs):** These networks possess a memory of previous inputs, making them ideal for sequential data like time series or natural language.

**Generative Adversarial Networks (GANs):** Comprising two networks (a generator and a discriminator), GANs can generate new data that resembles a given dataset.

## Applications of Deep Learning:

**Image and Video Recognition:** From tagging friends on social media to detecting tumors in medical scans, DL powers image recognition.

**Natural Language Processing:** Chatbots, translators, and sentiment analysis tools leverage DL to understand and generate human language.

**Voice Assistants:** Siri, Alexa, and Google Assistant use deep learning to understand and respond to user commands.

**Autonomous Vehicles:** Deep learning helps self-driving cars interpret their surroundings and make decisions.

**Challenges and Considerations:** Deep learning models, while powerful, require vast amounts of data and computational power. They can also sometimes act as "black boxes," making it hard to interpret their decisions. Ethical considerations, especially in areas like facial recognition, are paramount.

# Q-learning and Deep Q Networks in Reinforcement Learning

In the vast landscape of machine learning, there's a special corner dedicated to teaching machines not just to learn, but to act. This is the realm of Reinforcement Learning (RL), where agents learn to make decisions by interacting with an environment. Among the stars of this domain are Q-learning and its more sophisticated sibling, the Deep Q Network (DQN).

**Introduction to Q-learning**

Q-learning is a model-free reinforcement learning algorithm used to find the optimal action-selection policy for a given finite Markov decision process. In simpler terms, it helps an agent (like a robot or drone) learn how to choose optimal actions that yield the most reward over time, even when it doesn't know anything about its environment.

**The Essence of Q-learning**

At the heart of Q-learning is the Q-function, which calculates the expected reward for all possible actions in all possible states. The agent then uses this function to choose the action that will give it the maximum future reward.

**Mathematical Dive: The Q-function**

The Q-function is represented as $Q(s,a)$, where $s$ is a state and $a$ is an action. The function estimates the expected future reward of taking action $a$ in state $s$. The Q-function is updated using the Bellman equation:

$$Q(s,a)=r+\gamma \max a' Q(s',a')$$

Where:

- $r$ is the immediate reward after taking action $a$ in state $s$.

- $\gamma$ is the discount factor, representing the agent's consideration for future rewards. A high $\gamma$ makes the agent prioritize long-term reward over short-term reward.

- $s'$ is the next state after taking action $a$ in state $s$.

- $a'$ is the next action.

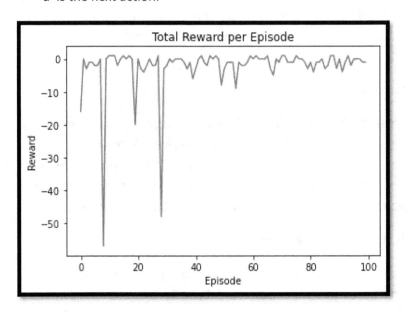

## Deep Q Networks (DQN)

While Q-learning is powerful, it has limitations, especially when dealing with large or continuous state spaces. Enter Deep Q Networks (DQN), which combine the power of deep neural networks with Q-learning.

**How DQN Works**

1. **Neural Network as Approximator:** Instead of a traditional Q-table, DQN uses a neural network to approximate the Q-function.

2. **Experience Replay:** DQN stores each state, action, reward, and next state in memory. Random batches from this memory are used to train the network, breaking the correlation between consecutive experiences.

3. **Target Network:** To stabilize training, DQN uses two networks: one to determine the current action and another to evaluate it.

## Applications

- **Gaming:** Both Q-learning and DQN have been used to train agents to play and often excel in complex games, from classic ones like Chess and Go to modern video games.

- **Robotics:** In tasks like navigation and object manipulation, these algorithms help robots learn optimal sequences of actions.

- **Finance:** In portfolio management and trading strategies, they can be used to maximize financial returns over time.

## Conclusion

Q-learning and Deep Q Networks represent a fascinating intersection of decision theory, game theory, optimization, and deep learning. They offer a glimpse into a future where machines don't just learn from data but also interact, explore, and make decisions in complex environments. Whether it's a drone navigating a forest, a financial system making trading decisions, or a video game character devising strategies, the principles of Q-learning and DQN are reshaping the boundaries of what machines can achieve.

# Natural Language Processing (NLP)

**Conversing with Computers**

Have you ever marveled at how Siri understands your requests? Or how Google Translate can seamlessly translate entire paragraphs into another language? The magic behind these feats is Natural Language Processing (NLP). Let's dive into the world where machines understand and generate human language.

**What is Natural Language Processing?**

NLP is a branch of artificial intelligence that focuses on the interaction between computers and humans through natural language. Its ultimate objective is to read, decipher, understand, and make sense of human language in a manner that is valuable.

**The Journey of NLP**

1. **Tokenization:** Breaking down text into words, phrases, symbols, or other meaningful elements (tokens) to understand its structure.

2. **Parsing:** Analyzing the grammatical structure of a sentence to extract meaning.

3. **Sentiment Analysis:** Determining the mood or subjective opinions within large amounts of text, such as positive, negative, or neutral sentiments.

4. **Machine Translation:** Translating text from one language to another automatically.

5. **Speech Recognition:** Converting spoken language into written text.

**Types of NLP Tasks**

**Information Retrieval:** Searching and retrieving relevant information from large databases, like search engines.

**Text Classification:** Categorizing text into predefined groups. For instance, identifying emails as spam or not spam.

**Named Entity Recognition:** Identifying and classifying named entities in text, such as names of people, places, dates, and more.

**Automatic Summarization:** Producing a concise and fluent summary while preserving key information content and overall meaning.

## Deep Learning in NLP

With the advent of deep learning, NLP has witnessed transformative changes. Recurrent Neural Networks (RNNs) and Transformers, like BERT (Bidirectional Encoder Representations from Transformers), have set new standards in tasks like machine translation and sentiment analysis.

## Applications of NLP

**Chatbots and Virtual Assistants:** Siri, Alexa, and Google Assistant use NLP to understand and respond to user queries.

**Content Recommendation:** Platforms like Netflix and Spotify analyze user reviews and feedback using NLP to recommend movies or songs.

**Healthcare:** NLP tools read and interpret clinical data, aiding in diagnosis and treatment suggestions.

## Challenges in NLP

Language is intricate and nuanced. Sarcasm, humor, cultural contexts, and evolving slang make NLP a challenging domain. Moreover, languages are diverse, and building comprehensive models for each is a monumental task.

Natural Language Processing is the bridge between machines and the essence of human communication: language. As technology advances, this bridge becomes stronger, paving the way for more intuitive and human-like interactions with machines. From simplifying tasks to breaking language barriers, NLP is reshaping the way we interact with technology.

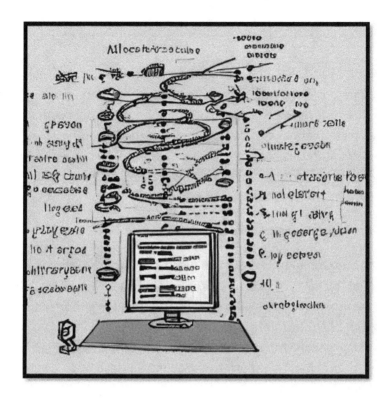

# Transformers in AI

The world of artificial intelligence (AI) and machine learning (ML) is vast, with numerous algorithms and architectures driving innovation. Among these, the "transformer" architecture stands out as a revolutionary development that has significantly impacted the field, especially in tasks related to natural language processing (NLP). This chapter delves into the world of transformers, exploring their origins, workings, and the transformative impact they've had on AI.

## Introduction to Transformers

The transformer architecture, introduced in the paper "Attention Is All You Need" by Vaswani et al. in 2017, presented a novel approach to handling sequential data without relying on traditional recurrent layers. At its core, the transformer leverages the concept of "attention" to draw global dependencies between input and output, allowing it to process data in parallel rather than sequentially, leading to significant speed-ups.

## The Magic of Attention

The attention mechanism is the heart of the transformer. It allows the model to focus on different parts of the input data with varying degrees of attention, akin to how humans pay attention to specific words when comprehending a sentence. This selective focus enables transformers to capture long-range dependencies in data, something that was challenging for previous architectures like RNNs and LSTMs.

## Key Components of Transformers

**Multi-Head Attention**: Instead of having a single set of attention weights, transformers use multiple sets, allowing them to capture different types of relationships in the data simultaneously.

**Positional Encoding**: Since transformers don't process data sequentially, they need a way to consider the position of data points. Positional encodings are added to the embeddings at the input layer to provide this positional context.

**Feed-forward Neural Networks**: Each transformer block contains a feed-forward neural network that operates independently on each position.

**Normalization and Residual Connections**: These components ensure smooth training and better performance of the transformer architecture.

## Transformers in Action: BERT, GPT, and Beyond

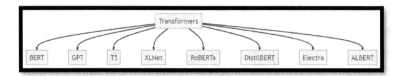

The transformer architecture has given rise to several state-of-the-art models, especially in NLP:

**BERT (Bidirectional Encoder Representations from Transformers)**: Introduced by Google, BERT captures context from both directions (left-to-right and right-to-left) and has set new benchmarks on several NLP tasks.

**GPT (Generative Pre-trained Transformer)**: Developed by OpenAI, GPT is designed to generate coherent and contextually relevant sentences and has shown remarkable capabilities in text generation tasks.

The success of these models has led to a flurry of research and the development of numerous transformer-based models tailored for various tasks beyond NLP, including computer vision and even bioinformatics.

### Challenges and the Road Ahead

While transformers have significantly advanced the field of AI, they are not without challenges:

**Computational Intensity**: Training transformer models, especially large ones, requires substantial computational resources.

**Model Interpretability**: The complex nature of transformers makes them harder to interpret compared to simpler models.

Despite these challenges, the future of transformers in AI looks promising. With continuous research and advancements, transformers are poised to remain at the forefront of AI innovations.

## Data, Data and more Data

Artificial Intelligence is by many considered a revolution in the same way as the internet changed the world. Promising to reshape industries, redefine customer experiences, and revolutionize problem-solving. However, the engine that powers this revolution is not just algorithms or computing power, it's data. Data serves as the lifeblood of AI systems, providing the raw material that these algorithms need to learn, adapt, and evolve. Without data, even the most sophisticated AI model is like a car without fuel—impressive to look at but incapable of going anywhere.

**Quality Over Quantity**

While it's tempting to think that more data automatically leads to better AI, the reality is more nuanced. The quality of data is equally, if not more, important than its quantity. Poor-quality data can lead to inaccurate predictions, biased outcomes, and ultimately, a loss of trust in AI systems. Therefore, organizations must invest in collecting high-quality, relevant data that aligns with the problem they are trying to solve.

## Different types of Data

**Structured Data**

Structured data is the type of data that most people are familiar with. It's organized, labeled, and easy to digest. Think of a spreadsheet where each column represents a different attribute, and each row represents a different record. This data is often numerical and fits neatly into tables. It's the go-to data type for problems that require clear, quantifiable insights, such as sales forecasting or customer segmentation.

**Unstructured Data**

Unstructured data is the opposite of structured data. It's messy, disorganized, and comes in various formats like text, images, and videos. This type of data doesn't fit neatly into tables but holds a wealth of information. Natural Language Processing (NLP) for text analysis, computer vision for image recognition, and deep learning techniques are often used to make sense of unstructured data.

**Time-Series Data**

Time-series data is a sequence of data points collected or recorded at specific time intervals. This data type is crucial for problems where temporal dynamics and trends play a significant role, such as stock price prediction or weather forecasting.

**Image and Video Data**

In tasks like object recognition, facial recognition, and medical imaging, the data comes in the form of images or videos. These data types require specialized algorithms, often based on neural networks, to analyze and interpret the visual information.

**Textual Data**

Textual data is pervasive in the age of the internet. From social media posts to customer reviews, this data type is rich in context but requires specialized techniques like NLP to extract meaningful insights.

**Audio Data**

Audio data is used in applications like speech recognition, music classification, and even diagnosing machinery based on the sounds they make. Like image and video data, audio data requires specialized algorithms for analysis.

**The combination of Data Types**

In real-world applications, it's common to encounter problems that require a mix of these data types. For example, a customer service AI might need to analyze textual data from customer emails, time-series data from customer interactions, and structured data from customer profiles to provide a comprehensive solution.

## Data collection and preprocessing

## Collecting data

Before any AI model can start learning, it needs data, and that data must come from somewhere. Data collection is the first critical step in any AI project, serving as the gateway between the real world and the digital realm where AI operates. But it's not just about gathering as much data as possible; it's about gathering the right kind of data.

Different AI projects require different types of data. For instance, a natural language processing model would need textual data, while a computer vision model would require image data. The source of this data can vary widely, from publicly available datasets and APIs to proprietary databases or even real-time sensor data.

### Ethics and Regulations

Ethical considerations also come into play during data collection. Ensuring that the data is collected in a manner that respects user privacy and consent is paramount. Regulations like GDPR in Europe and CCPA in California have set legal frameworks for data collection. Organizations are required to follow them when gathering data.

## Data Preprocessing

Once the data is collected, it's rare that it will be in a perfect state for immediate use in an AI model. Real-world data is messy. It can have missing values, outliers, or inconsistencies that need to be addressed. This is where data preprocessing comes in.

### Data Cleaning

The first step in preprocessing is often cleaning the data. This involves handling missing values, removing outliers, and correcting inconsistencies in the dataset. For example, if you're working with a dataset of customer ages, and one entry is 250 years (which is clearly an error), that would be considered an outlier and should be addressed.

### Data Transformation

After cleaning the data, the next step is usually transforming it into a format that will be more effective for training models. This can involve normalization (scaling all numerical variables to a standard range), encoding categorical variables, or even more complex transformations like Fourier transforms for time-series data.

**Feature Engineering**

Feature engineering is the art of selecting the most relevant features (or variables) to use in model training, or even creating new features from the existing ones. Good feature engineering can make the difference between a mediocre model and a great one.

**Data Augmentation**

In some cases, especially when dealing with image or audio data, data augmentation techniques can be applied to artificially increase the size of the training dataset. This can include techniques like rotating images, adding noise to audio clips, or generating new text samples.

## Annotation, Making Sense of Raw Data

Data annotation is the process of labelling or tagging raw data to make it understandable for machine learning algorithms. This is an essential step, especially for supervised learning models, where the algorithm learns from labelled examples. For instance, in a computer vision task, images might be annotated to identify objects within them. In natural language processing, sentences might be tagged to indicate the sentiment they express.

The quality of annotation directly impacts the performance of the AI model. Poorly annotated data can lead to inaccurate or biased models. Therefore, it's crucial to have a well-defined annotation process, which could be manual, semi-automated, or fully automated. Manual annotation often involves human experts who understand both the data and the problem domain, while automated methods can use pre-existing models to annotate new data.

**Labelling The basis Supervised Learning**

Labelling is a specific type of annotation used mainly in supervised learning. In this context, "labels" are the outcomes or the "answers" that the model aims to predict. For example, in a spam detection model, emails would be labelled as either "spam" or "not spam." The model uses these labels during training to learn the characteristics of spam and non-spam emails.

## Data Splitting

Once the data is annotated and labelled, the next crucial step is data splitting. This involves dividing the dataset into multiple subsets to facilitate different phases of the machine learning process. The most common practice is to split the data into three sets:

1. **Training Set**: This is the largest subset, often making up 60-80% of the dataset. The training set is used to train the model, allowing it to learn from the data's features and labels.

2. **Validation Set**: This set is used to fine-tune model parameters and to provide an unbiased evaluation of the model during the training phase. It usually makes up about 10-20% of the dataset.

3. **Test Set**: This is the subset of data that the model has never seen during its training or validation phases. It's used to assess how well the model will perform on unseen data and usually makes up the remaining 10-20% of the dataset.

The splitting is often done randomly but can also be stratified to ensure that each subset has a similar distribution of labels. This is particularly important for imbalanced datasets.

## Pre-existing Datasets

In the world of AI and machine learning, data is often considered the new oil. However, collecting, annotating, and preprocessing data can be a time-consuming and costly affair. This is where existing datasets come into play. These are collections of data that have already been gathered, and often annotated, for specific tasks or general research. Leveraging these datasets can significantly accelerate the development cycle of AI projects.

**Types of Existing Datasets**

Existing datasets can be broadly categorized into:

**Public Datasets**: These are freely available datasets often released by academic institutions, government organizations, or even private companies for research and development. Examples include the UCI Machine Learning Repository, Kaggle datasets, and government databases like the U.S. Census data.

**Commercial Datasets**: These are datasets that are available for purchase or licensing. They are often highly specialized and come with a certain level of guarantee regarding their quality and reliability.

**In-house Datasets**: Larger organizations often have internal datasets from previous projects that can be repurposed or combined to create a new dataset for a different AI application.

**Where to Find Them**

Several platforms and repositories offer a wide range of datasets for various AI tasks:

- **Kaggle**: A platform for data science competitions that also offers a variety of public datasets.

- **UCI Machine Learning Repository**: A well-known repository that provides datasets specifically tailored for machine learning.

- **European open data portal**: More than one million datasets available from the over 30 countries in Europe.

- **Data.gov**: A comprehensive resource offering public datasets including everything from climate data to high-quality healthcare data.

- **AWS Data Exchange**: A marketplace for datasets, which includes both free and paid options.

- **Google Dataset Search Engine**: Makes it possible to search thousands of different datasets repositories.

- **VisualData**: A collection of datasets for training computer vision models.

## Ethical and Legal Considerations

While existing datasets offer convenience, it's essential to consider the ethical and legal implications of their use. Always check the licensing terms to ensure you have the right to use the dataset for your intended purpose. Also, be aware of any biases that may exist in the data, as these can propagate through your AI models.

# Typical Problems When Creating Artificial Intelligence

## Overfitting

Overfitting is one of the most common and critical challenges faced in the realm of machine learning and artificial intelligence. It's a phenomenon that can drastically reduce the effectiveness of a model, rendering it almost useless in real-world scenarios, despite showing promising results during training. In this section, we delve deep into the concept of overfitting, its causes, consequences, and the strategies to combat it.

**What is Overfitting?**

At its core, overfitting occurs when a machine learning model learns the training data too well, including its noise and outliers. As a result, while it may achieve high accuracy on the training data, it performs poorly on new, unseen data. Essentially, the model becomes an "overachiever" in memorizing the training data, failing to generalize to new situations.

**Causes of Overfitting**

**Complex Models**: A model with excessive complexity, such as a deep neural network with too many layers or a polynomial regression of a very high degree, can easily fit every nuance of the training data, including the noise.

**Insufficient Data**: A small dataset might not capture the entire spectrum of the problem, leading the model to memorize rather than generalize.

**Noisy Data**: If the training data contains errors or irrelevant information, the model might learn these as patterns.

**Redundant Features**: Features that don't contribute to the predictive power can lead the model astray.

**Detecting Overfitting**

The most straightforward way to detect overfitting is by comparing the model's performance on the training data with its performance on a validation set. A significant discrepancy in performance is a red flag.

**Mitigating Overfitting**

**Regularization**: Techniques like L1 (Lasso) and L2 (Ridge) regularization add a penalty to the model's complexity, discouraging it from relying too heavily on any single feature.

**Cross-Validation**: By partitioning the training data and training the model multiple times on different partitions, one can get a better sense of how the model might perform on unseen data.

**Pruning**: In tree-based algorithms, pruning helps by removing branches that have little predictive power.

**Early Stopping**: Especially useful in deep learning, training can be halted as soon as the model's performance on a validation set starts deteriorating.

**Data Augmentation**: For tasks like image recognition, slightly altering the training data (like rotating images) can help the model generalize better.

**Simplifying the Model**: Sometimes, a less complex model might be more effective. For instance, using a linear regression instead of a polynomial one.

**The Balance Between Bias and Variance**

Overfitting is closely related to the concepts of bias and variance in machine learning. High variance often leads to overfitting, where the model is too flexible and fits the training data's noise. On the other hand, high bias results in underfitting, where the model is too rigid to capture the data's patterns. Striking the right balance is crucial for an effective model.

## Conclusion

Overfitting is a formidable challenge in AI, but with awareness and the right techniques, it's a hurdle that can be overcome. Ensuring that a model generalizes well to new data is paramount to harnessing the true potential of AI in real-world applications.

## Underfitting

While the world of machine learning often buzzes with concerns about overfitting, its lesser-discussed counterpart, underfitting, is equally detrimental. Underfitting is the shadow lurking in the background, representing models that, for various reasons, fail to capture the essence of the data they're trained on. In this section, we'll explore the concept of underfitting, its causes, consequences, and ways to address it.

### What is Underfitting?

Underfitting occurs when a machine learning model is too simplistic to grasp or represent the underlying structure of the data. Such a model tends to have poor predictive performance, not just on new, unseen data, but also on the training data itself. In essence, the model fails to "learn" from the data, leading to generalized and often inaccurate predictions.

### Causes of Underfitting

**Simplistic Models**: Using a model that lacks the complexity needed to understand the data patterns can lead to underfitting. For instance, using a linear regression model for inherently non-linear data.

**Overly Strict Regularization**: While regularization helps prevent overfitting, being too aggressive with it can strip the model of its capacity to learn from data.

**Insufficient Features**: Not providing the model with enough information or features about the data can hinder its learning capability.

**Poor Quality Data**: If the training data lacks variability or is too homogeneous, the model might not get enough diverse examples to learn effectively.

### Detecting Underfitting

Underfitting can be identified by observing the model's performance metrics. A model that underfits will have poor accuracy, precision, recall, or other relevant metrics on both the training and validation datasets.

### Addressing Underfitting

**Increasing Model Complexity**: If the current model is too simple, consider switching to a more complex model or architecture. For instance, moving from linear regression to polynomial regression.

**Feature Engineering**: Introducing new features or transforming existing ones can provide the model with more information to learn from.

**Reducing Regularization**: If regularization is applied, consider reducing its intensity or removing it altogether.

**More Data**: Sometimes, providing more diverse training examples can help, especially if the current dataset is too small or lacks variability.

**Hyperparameter Tuning**: Adjusting the model's hyperparameters, such as the learning rate, can sometimes help the model learn better.

## The Balance Revisited

Just as with overfitting, underfitting also relates to the bias-variance trade-off. High bias leads to underfitting, where the model's assumptions are too strong to adapt to the data's nuances. On the other hand, high variance leads to overfitting. Achieving a balance between the two is crucial for optimal model performance.

## Conclusion

Underfitting, though less discussed than overfitting, is a significant challenge in machine learning. It represents missed opportunities, where models fail to harness the rich information present in the data. By recognizing and addressing underfitting, practitioners can ensure that their AI models are not just memorizing, but truly understanding and learning from the data they're presented with.

## Data Imbalance

It's a subtle issue, often overlooked, but with profound implications on the performance and fairness of machine learning models. This section delves into the intricacies of data imbalance, its repercussions, and strategies to address it.

**What is Data Imbalance?**

Data imbalance refers to a situation where certain classes in a classification problem are underrepresented compared to others. In simpler terms, one class has significantly more samples than the other(s). This disproportion in class distribution can lead to biased models that favor the majority class, often at the expense of the minority class.

**Why is Data Imbalance a Problem?**

**Model Bias**: A model trained on imbalanced data tends to be biased towards the majority class. It might achieve high accuracy by simply predicting the majority class for all inputs.

**Poor Generalization**: Such models often fail to generalize well to real-world scenarios where the class distribution might be different.

**Misleading Metrics**: High accuracy doesn't always indicate a good model, especially with imbalanced data. A model predicting only the majority class can still achieve high accuracy if the majority class is predominant.

**Ethical Concerns**: In certain applications, like medical diagnosis or credit approval, overlooking the minority class can have serious ethical and practical implications.

**Techniques to Address Data Imbalance**

**Resampling:**

**Oversampling**: This involves increasing the number of

instances in the minority class by replicating them or generating synthetic samples using methods like SMOTE (Synthetic Minority Over-sampling Technique).

**Undersampling**: This involves reducing the number of instances in the majority class, either randomly or using structured methods.

**Using Different Evaluation Metrics**: Instead of accuracy, metrics like precision, recall, F1-score, and the area under the ROC curve (AUC-ROC) can provide a more holistic view of model performance.

**Cost-sensitive Learning**: Assigning higher misclassification costs to the minority class can make the model more attentive to it.

**Ensemble Methods**: Techniques like bagging and boosting, when combined with resampling, can help in improving the performance on the minority class.

**Anomaly Detection**: Treating the minority class as an anomaly detection problem can sometimes yield better results.

### Real-world Implications

Data imbalance is not just a theoretical concern. In real-world applications, from finance to healthcare, the repercussions of not addressing data imbalance can be severe. For instance, a model trained to detect rare diseases might overlook them if the training data is imbalanced, leading to missed diagnoses.

### The Bigger Picture: Fairness in AI

Data imbalance ties into the broader theme of fairness in AI. A model's bias towards the majority class can perpetuate existing biases in data, leading to unfair and discriminatory outcomes. Addressing data imbalance is a step towards building more equitable AI systems.

### Conclusion

Data imbalance, while seemingly a technical concern, has deep-rooted implications on the efficacy and ethics of AI systems. Recognizing and addressing this imbalance is paramount for building models that are not only accurate but also fair and reliable. As AI continues to permeate various sectors of society, ensuring that it works equitably for everyone becomes all the more crucial.

## Lack of Interpretability, Model Drift, and High Dimensionality

Other common issues when working with data and AI models are the lack of interpretability, model drift, and the curse of high dimensionality. Here we investigate these challenges, shedding light on their implications and offering strategies to navigate them.

### Lack of Interpretability

**Understanding the Issue**: Interpretability refers to the extent to which a human can understand the decision-making process of a model. Many advanced ML models, especially deep neural networks, are often termed as "black boxes" due to their complex architectures and lack of transparency in how they arrive at decisions.

**Implications**

Trust: It's challenging to trust a model whose decisions cannot be explained or understood.

**Regulatory Concerns**: In sectors like finance and healthcare, regulators demand explanations for algorithmic decisions.

**Debugging**: Without interpretability, diagnosing and fixing model errors becomes a daunting task.

**Navigating the Challenge**:

**Model-specific Techniques**: Some models, like decision trees or linear regression, are inherently interpretable.

**Post-hoc Interpretation**: Techniques like LIME (Local Interpretable Model-agnostic Explanations) or SHAP (SHapley Additive exPlanations) can be used to explain black-box models after they have been trained.

## Model Drift

**Understanding the Issue**: Model drift, or concept drift, refers to the change in data distribution over time, causing the model's performance to degrade.

**Implications**

**Reduced Accuracy**: As the underlying data changes, models can become less accurate and reliable.

**Relevance**: Models might become outdated, making decisions based on old patterns.

**Navigating the Challenge**:

**Continuous Monitoring**: Regularly monitor the model's performance against fresh data.

**Incremental Learning**: Train models in an online fashion, allowing them to adapt to new data patterns.

**Feedback Loops**: Implement systems where human experts can correct the model, allowing it to learn from its mistakes.

## High Dimensionality

**Understanding the Issue**: High dimensionality, often referred to as the "curse of dimensionality," arises when data has a large number of features or dimensions.

### Implications

**Overfitting**: With more features, models can easily fit noise in the training data, leading to overfitting.

**Computational Complexity**: Processing high-dimensional data requires more computational resources.

**Reduced Intuition**: Visualizing and understanding data in high dimensions is challenging.

### Navigating the Challenge

**Dimensionality Reduction**: Techniques like Principal Component Analysis (PCA) or t-SNE can reduce the number of dimensions while retaining most of the information.

**Feature Selection**: Instead of using all features, select a subset that contributes the most to the predictive power.

**Regularization**: Techniques like Lasso regression can help in feature selection by adding penalties for using more features.

## Other noteworthy challenges in AI

The journey of AI is not without its fair share of hurdles. Beyond the primary challenges discussed, several other complexities often arise in the realm of AI.

**Data privacy and security** have become paramount as AI models often require vast amounts of data. Breaches can lead to a loss of trust, legal repercussions, and harm to individuals whose data is compromised. As datasets grow and models become more intricate, ensuring that systems can scale to handle this growth becomes crucial. Without scalability, models can become slow, inefficient, or entirely unfeasible.

**Bias and fairness** present another significant challenge. AI models can inadvertently learn and perpetuate biases present in their training data, leading to unfair or discriminatory outcomes, especially in sensitive areas like hiring or lending. The challenge of ensuring that a model trained on one dataset performs well on other, unseen datasets is persistent. Models that fail to generalize might perform poorly in real-world scenarios, even if they excel during training.

**Hardware limitations** also come into play, especially as advanced models, particularly deep learning architectures, often require specialized hardware like GPUs. This need can increase the cost and complexity of deploying AI solutions. Moving a model from a development environment to a production setting and ensuring its continuous performance is non-trivial. Models might face issues in production that weren't apparent during development, leading to reduced effectiveness or system downtimes.

# AI Applications. Transforming Everyday Life

## The AI Revolution: Beyond the Lab and Into the World

Artificial Intelligence, once a subject of science fiction, has now permeated every facet of our lives. From healthcare to entertainment, AI's applications are vast and transformative. Let's explore some ways in which AI is reshaping industries and enhancing our daily experiences.

## Computer Vision

### Seeing Through the Eyes of Machines

Imagine a world where computers can not only see but also understand and interpret what they're seeing. From recognizing faces in a crowd to detecting defects in manufacturing lines, computer vision is revolutionizing the way machines interact with the visual world. Let's delve into this fascinating domain where machines gain the power of sight.

### What is Computer Vision?

Computer Vision (CV) is a field of artificial intelligence that trains machines to interpret and make decisions based on visual data. It's akin to bestowing machines with a visual cortex, enabling them to recognize, process, and understand visual information similarly to humans.

### The Process of Computer Vision:

1. **Image Acquisition:** Capturing visual data using cameras or sensors.

2. **Preprocessing:** Enhancing the image quality by removing noise, adjusting contrast, or other techniques.

3. **Feature Extraction:** Identifying and extracting key features from the image, like edges, textures, or colors.

4. **Detection & Recognition:** Identifying objects, patterns, or specific features within the image.

5. **Post-processing:** Refining the detection results to improve accuracy.

6. **Analysis & Interpretation:** Understanding the context and making decisions based on the visual data.

## Types of Computer Vision Tasks

**Image Classification:** Categorizing an image into one of several predefined classes.

**Object Detection:** Identifying specific objects within an image and their locations.

**Image Segmentation:** Dividing an image into multiple segments, each representing a different object or part of the scene.

**Facial Recognition:** Identifying or verifying a person based on their facial features.

**Optical Character Recognition (OCR):** Converting images of typed or handwritten text into machine-readable text.

## Deep Learning in Computer Vision

Deep learning, especially Convolutional Neural Networks (CNNs), has been a game-changer for computer vision. CNNs can automatically learn hierarchical features from images, leading to breakthroughs in tasks like image classification and object detection.

## Applications of Computer Vision

**Healthcare:** From detecting tumors in X-rays to analyzing cell images, CV aids in diagnosis and treatment.

**Autonomous Vehicles:** Self-driving cars use computer vision to navigate, detect obstacles, and interpret traffic signs.

**Retail:** Automated checkout systems, customer behavior analysis, and inventory management are enhanced with CV.

**Agriculture:** Drones equipped with cameras monitor crops, analyze soil health, and detect pests using computer vision.

## Challenges in Computer Vision

While CV has made significant strides, challenges remain. Variability in lighting, occlusions, diverse perspectives, and real-time processing requirements can make computer vision tasks complex. Moreover, ethical concerns, especially in surveillance and facial recognition, require careful consideration.

## Adaptive Learning Platforms

**Personalizing Education for Every Learner**

Remember the days when learning was confined to a one-size-fits-all approach? Rows of desks, a standard curriculum, and everyone moving at the same pace. Enter Adaptive Learning Platforms, the game-changers in education, tailoring learning experiences to individual needs. Let's explore how technology is making education more personal, dynamic, and effective.

**What are Adaptive Learning Platforms?**

Adaptive Learning Platforms are technology-driven educational systems designed to adjust the content, resources, and learning pathways in real-time based on individual student performance and needs. Think of it as a personal tutor embedded in a digital platform, understanding a student's strengths, weaknesses, and pace, and then providing content accordingly.

**How Do They Work?**

1. **Data Collection:** The platform continuously collects data on a student's interactions, responses, time taken, and more.

2. **Analysis:** Advanced algorithms and AI analyze this data to understand the student's learning style, proficiency, and areas of struggle.

3. **Personalization:** Based on the analysis, the platform adapts the content, offering more challenging tasks, revisiting foundational concepts, or even changing the learning modality (e.g., from text to video).

**Key Features of Adaptive Learning Platforms**

**Personalized Learning Paths:** Custom-tailored sequences of topics and tasks based on individual progress and understanding.

**Instant Feedback:** Immediate responses to student inputs, helping them understand mistakes and correct them in real-time.

**Dynamic Content Adjustment:** Changing the difficulty level, type, or modality of content based on student performance.

**Progress Tracking:** Detailed analytics and reports on a student's journey, highlighting achievements and areas for improvement.

**Collaborative Learning:** Some platforms integrate social learning features, allowing students to collaborate, discuss, and learn from peers.

## Benefits of Adaptive Learning Platforms

**Efficiency:** Students spend time on what they need to learn, not what they already know.

**Engagement:** Dynamic and interactive content keeps students engaged and motivated.

**Flexibility:** Learning at one's own pace, anytime, anywhere.

**Improved Outcomes:** Personalized attention often leads to better understanding and retention.

## Applications in the Real World

**K-12 Education:** Enhancing classroom learning by providing teachers with insights and students with personalized content.

**Higher Education:** Offering college students adaptive courses that cater to diverse backgrounds and knowledge levels.

**Corporate Training:** Tailoring training modules based on employee roles, experience, and performance.

**Skill Development:** Platforms that offer courses on specific skills, adapting to the learner's progress.

## Challenges and Considerations

While adaptive learning platforms offer numerous advantages, they also come with challenges. Data privacy concerns, the digital divide (not all students have equal access to technology), and over-reliance on technology are issues that educators and developers must address.

## Predictive Maintenance

**The Proactive Approach to Equipment Health**

In the intricate dance of machinery and production lines, unexpected breakdowns can be costly missteps. Predictive Maintenance steps in as the vigilant overseer, ensuring that machines operate smoothly and that potential issues are addressed before they escalate.

**What is Predictive Maintenance?**

Predictive Maintenance (PdM) employs data-driven tools and techniques to monitor equipment health continuously. By predicting potential failures, it allows for timely maintenance interventions, reducing unplanned downtimes and extending the lifespan of the equipment.

**The Mechanics of Predictive Maintenance**

1. **Data Collection:** Sensors affixed to machinery gather data in real-time, monitoring metrics like temperature, vibration, and humidity.

2. **Data Analysis:** Sophisticated algorithms, often underpinned by machine learning, sift through this data to discern patterns and anomalies.

3. **Prediction:** Leveraging both historical and real-time data, the system forecasts when a piece of equipment might fail.

4. **Action:** Maintenance activities are strategically scheduled based on these predictions, ensuring equipment remains in optimal condition with minimal disruption.

**Key Components of Predictive Maintenance**

**Sensors:** These devices are integral for collecting real-time data from machinery.

**Data Aggregation Tools:** Systems designed to amass data from diverse sources, prepping it for analysis.

**Analytical Software:** Tools dedicated to data analysis, pattern recognition, and making informed predictions.

**User Interface:** Dashboards that present insights, predictive data, and recommended actions to users.

## Benefits of Predictive Maintenance

**Reduced Downtime:** By pre-emptively identifying potential failures, unplanned outages become rare occurrences.

**Cost Efficiency:** Maintenance is executed only when necessary, curbing superfluous expenses.

**Prolonged Equipment Life:** Regular and timely maintenance often correlates with longer machinery lifespan.

**Safety Enhancement:** Predicting and preventing failures can bolster workplace safety.

**Operational Optimization:** Consistent operations and fewer disruptions lead to heightened productivity.

## Applications in the Real World

**Manufacturing:** Overseeing machinery on production lines to preempt and avert malfunctions.

**Energy:** Monitoring essential components like turbines, generators, and transformers in power plants.

**Transportation:** Keeping a close watch on aircraft engines, train systems, and fleet vehicles to ensure peak performance.

**Healthcare:** Anticipating the maintenance requirements of vital apparatus such as MRI machines and ventilators.

## Challenges and Considerations

While the advantages of Predictive Maintenance are manifold, its implementation is not without hurdles. Initial investments in technology and training are prerequisites. Ensuring data privacy and security, especially in cloud-based systems, is crucial. The efficacy of predictions hinges on the quality of data and the precision of algorithms, necessitating ongoing refinement.

## Autonomous Systems and Self-Driving Cars

**Navigating the Future on Autopilot**

As technology propels us into the future, the vision of vehicles navigating bustling streets without human intervention is becoming a reality. Autonomous systems, especially self-driving cars, are at the forefront of this revolution, promising a future of safer, more efficient, and accessible transportation.

**What are Autonomous Systems?**

Autonomous systems refer to machines or devices that can perform tasks or make decisions without direct human control. These systems combine sensors, algorithms, and actuators to interact with their environment and carry out their functions. From drones to robotic vacuum cleaners, autonomous systems are becoming an integral part of our daily lives.

**The Rise of Self-Driving Cars**

Self-driving cars, also known as autonomous vehicles (AVs), are equipped with sensors, cameras, and advanced algorithms that allow them to navigate roads and make driving decisions without human input.

**Levels of Automation**

**Level 0 (No Automation):** The human driver is responsible for all driving tasks.

**Level 1 (Driver Assistance):** Single automation system, like cruise control.

**Level 2 (Partial Automation):** The vehicle can control both steering and acceleration/deceleration using information about the driving environment.

**Level 3 (Conditional Automation):** The vehicle can handle some driving tasks, but the human driver must be ready to take control.

**Level 4 (High Automation):** The vehicle can handle most driving situations independently, but might need human intervention in more complex scenarios.

**Level 5 (Full Automation):** The vehicle can handle all driving tasks under all conditions.

## Benefits of Self-Driving Cars

**Safety:** Autonomous vehicles have the potential to reduce accidents caused by human error, such as distracted or impaired driving.

**Efficiency:** Optimized traffic flow and reduced congestion due to coordinated vehicle movement.

**Accessibility:** Providing mobility solutions for individuals who cannot drive, such as the elderly or disabled.

**Environmental Impact:** Potential for reduced emissions with optimized driving patterns and increased adoption of electric vehicles.

## Challenges and Considerations

**Technological Limitations:** Ensuring that AVs can handle all driving scenarios, especially in unpredictable conditions.

**Ethical Dilemmas:** Programming decisions for scenarios where harm is unavoidable.

**Regulatory and Legal Issues:** Establishing laws and regulations for testing and deploying AVs.

**Job Displacement:** Impact on professions related to driving, such as truckers and taxi drivers.

## The Road Ahead

While the promise of self-driving cars is immense, the road to full autonomy is filled with challenges. Collaboration between tech companies, automakers, regulators, and the public is crucial to ensure that the transition to this new era of transportation is smooth and beneficial for all.

## Traffic Management with AI

**The Congestion Conundrum**

Urban centers around the world grapple with traffic congestion, a challenge that not only leads to frustrated drivers but also has broader implications for the environment, economy, and public health. As cities grow and vehicles become more prevalent, traditional traffic management systems are proving inadequate. Enter Artificial Intelligence (AI) – a game-changer in the realm of urban traffic management.

**How AI is Revolutionizing Traffic Management**

1. **Real-time Traffic Analysis and Prediction:**

   **Description:** AI algorithms analyze data from traffic cameras, sensors, and social media to monitor traffic conditions in real-time. These systems can predict traffic jams before they occur by analyzing patterns and considering factors like weather, events, or roadwork.

   **Use Case:** Alerting drivers about potential traffic hotspots, allowing them to choose alternative routes.

2. **Smart Traffic Signals:**

   **Description:** Traditional traffic lights operate on fixed timers, but AI-driven traffic signals adapt to real-time traffic conditions. By analyzing the flow of traffic, these signals can optimize green light durations to reduce waiting times and improve traffic flow.

   **Use Case:** Busy intersections where traditional fixed-timer signals lead to long waiting times and congestion.

3. **Pedestrian and Cyclist Safety:**

   **Description:** AI systems can detect pedestrians and cyclists, adjusting traffic signals accordingly to ensure their safety.

**Use Case:** Busy urban areas with high pedestrian traffic, especially near schools, parks, or shopping districts.

4. **Parking Solutions:**

   **Description:** AI-powered cameras and sensors can identify available parking spaces in real-time and relay this information to drivers.

   **Use Case:** Crowded urban centers where finding parking is a challenge, reducing the need for drivers to circle around searching for a spot.

5. **Public Transport Optimization:**

   **Description:** AI can analyze passenger data, traffic conditions, and other variables to optimize public transport routes and schedules.

   **Use Case:** Ensuring buses and trams run efficiently during peak hours, special events, or emergencies.

6. **Emergency Response Coordination:**

   **Description:** In the event of emergencies, AI systems can coordinate traffic signals to create clear routes for emergency vehicles.

   **Use Case:** Ensuring ambulances, fire trucks, and police vehicles reach their destinations without delays.

**The Broader Impact of AI in Traffic Management**

**Environmental Benefits:** Efficient traffic flow reduces idling and congestion, leading to decreased vehicle emissions.

**Economic Advantages:** Reducing traffic congestion can lead to significant economic savings by decreasing fuel consumption and increasing productivity.

**Enhanced Quality of Life:** Less time spent in traffic means more time for personal and recreational activities, leading to improved well-being.

## Challenges and Considerations

While AI holds immense promise in revolutionizing traffic management, it's essential to consider potential challenges:

**Data Privacy:** The extensive use of cameras and sensors raises concerns about individual privacy and data security.

**Infrastructure Costs:** Upgrading traditional traffic systems to AI-powered ones requires significant investment.

**Reliability and Accuracy:** Ensuring that AI systems are reliable and accurate in diverse and dynamic urban environments is crucial.

# Ethics in AI. A Moral Labyrinth

The dawn of Artificial Intelligence (AI) has brought about a transformative shift in our world. Its capabilities touch every domain, from healthcare to finance. Yet, as we stand at this technological crossroads, the ethical implications of AI loom large, demanding our attention and thoughtful navigation.

**The Ethical Challenges**

**Bias and Fairness:** AI's potential to inadvertently perpetuate societal biases is a significant concern. When trained on skewed data, these systems can lead to discriminatory outcomes in various sectors, with marginalized groups often bearing the brunt of such biases.

**Transparency and Accountability:** The intricate, often opaque workings of AI models challenge our understanding of their decision-making processes. This "black box" nature complicates efforts to hold these systems and their creators accountable.

**Privacy Concerns:** With AI's integration into surveillance tools, there's a heightened risk of intruding on individual privacy. The collection and analysis of personal data without clear consent raise pressing concerns about personal rights and potential misuse.

**Economic Impacts:** AI-driven automation threatens job displacement across diverse sectors. The resulting economic disparities and potential societal unrest underscore the need for foresight and planning.

**Safety and Weaponization:** As AI takes on more critical roles, from autonomous driving to medical diagnoses, the stakes for potential malfunctions rise. Additionally, the prospect of AI's weaponization, especially in autonomous weapons, presents grave ethical dilemmas.

**Guiding the AI Ethical Journey**

To address these challenges, we must adhere to certain guiding principles:

**Inclusivity:** Promoting diversity in AI development can help in curbing biases and fostering more equitable systems.

**Commitment to Transparency:** Demystifying AI models and their decision-making processes can pave the way for greater trust and understanding.

**Accountability:** Clear guidelines and frameworks can ensure responsibility is assigned when AI systems falter.

**User Privacy:** Prioritizing and safeguarding user privacy is paramount, especially in an era where data is the new gold.

**Continuous Oversight:** Regular monitoring and updating of AI systems can ensure they remain aligned with evolving ethical standards.

**Conclusion**

The journey of AI is as much an ethical one as it is technological. By embracing a collaborative approach involving technologists, ethicists, policymakers, and the public, we can ensure AI's evolution is grounded in our shared values. The goal is a future where AI not only augments our capabilities but also respects and upholds our moral compass.

# The Future of AI

As we navigate the transformative age of Artificial Intelligence (AI), it's both exhilarating and essential to cast our gaze forward. The future of AI is not just about technological advancements but also about its profound implications on society, economy, and our daily lives.

## The Promise of Advanced AI

**General Artificial Intelligence (AGI):** The vision of a General AI, capable of performing any intellectual task that a human can, remains a tantalizing goal. Such an AI would not just replicate human tasks but think, learn, and adapt across diverse domains autonomously.

**Quantum Computing and AI:** Merging the power of quantum computing with AI promises computational speeds and capabilities beyond our current imagination. This combination could redefine fields ranging from cryptography to complex molecular simulations.

**Neuro-AI:** By intertwining insights from neuroscience with AI, there's potential to craft neural networks that mirror the human brain's intricacies. Such systems could offer more intuitive, adaptive, and efficient AI solutions.

**AI in Healthcare:** The future might see AI not just assisting doctors but predicting diseases before symptoms appear, personalizing treatments to individual genetic makeups, and revolutionizing drug discovery.

**Emotionally Intelligent AI:** Beyond logic and computation, efforts are underway to develop AI that can understand, interpret, and even replicate human emotions. Such systems could lead to more personalized user experiences and more nuanced human-AI interactions.

**Decentralized AI:** With the rise of blockchain and similar technologies, there's potential for AI systems that are decentralized, ensuring data privacy, security, and democratizing access to AI's benefits.

## Challenges and Considerations

**Ethical Implications:** The deeper integration of AI into our lives amplifies ethical dilemmas, from data privacy to the transparency of AI decisions. Striking a balance between innovation and ethics will be pivotal.

**Economic Impact:** While AI promises efficiency, it also poses the challenge of job displacement. Preemptive strategies, such as reskilling and continuous education, will be essential to navigate this shift.

**AI Governance:** The growing influence of AI necessitates robust global standards and regulatory frameworks. Proper governance will ensure AI's evolution is beneficial, safe, and equitable.

## The Human-AI Collaboration

The essence of the AI future lies in the symbiotic relationship between humans and machines. This partnership is set to augment human capabilities, foster creativity, and drive unprecedented innovations across sectors.

## Conclusion

The horizon of AI is vast, filled with promises and challenges. As we journey forward, a holistic approach—embracing collaboration, championing ethics, and fostering education—will be our guiding star. This approach ensures that AI's future is not just about technological marvels but also about enriching human experience.